Primary Sources in World History

THE REFORMATION

ENZO GEORGE

Cavendish
Square

New York

Published in 2017 by Cavendish Square Publishing, LLC
243 5th Avenue, Suite 136 New York, NY 10016

Website: cavendishsq.com

This publication represents the opinions and views of the author based on his or her personal experiences, knowledge, and research. The information in this book serves as a general guide only. The author and publisher have used their best efforts in preparing this book and disclaim liabilty rising directly or indirectly for the use and application of this book.

CPSIA compliance information: Batch #CS16CSQ.

All websites were available and accurate when this book went to press.

Library of Congress Cataloging-in-Publication Data

Names: George, Enzo.
Title: The Reformation / Enzo George.
Description: New York : Cavendish Square, 2016. | Series: Primary sources in world history | Includes index.
Identifiers: ISBN 9781502620163 (library bound) | ISBN 9781502620170 (ebook)
Subjects: LCSH: Reformation—Juvenile literature | Church history—Juvenile literature.
Classification: LCC BR308.G46 2016 | DDC 270.6—dc23

For Brown Bear Books Ltd:
Editorial Director: Lindsey Lowe
Managing Editor: Tim Cooke
Children's Publisher: Anne O'Daly
Design Manager: Keith Davis
Designer: Lynne Lennon
Picture Manager: Sophie Mortimer

Picture Credits:
Front Cover: Alamy: Prisma Archivo main; Shutterstock: ilolab map.
Interior: Bibliothèque de Genève: 32; British Museum: 33; Deutsches Historisches Museum: 43; Dreamstime: Mattphoto 6; Gallerie dell'Accademia: 39; Geoffrey Groesbeck: 30; Library of Congress: 9, 18, 19; Musée Cantonal des Beaux-Arts: 35; Museo di San Marco: 13; Museo Nacional del Prado: 10, 28; mutualart.com: ifc, 17; Real Academia de Bellas Artes: 11; Robert Hunt Library: 15, 25, 29, 40; Shutterstock: Everett Historical 31, 38, IR Stone 27, nomadFra 36, S-F 16, Jan Schneckenhaus 8, Michael Warwick 26; Spiezer Chronik: 7; St Bonaventure University: 12; Stecher/Verlenger: 42; Thinkstock: anshar73 22, Photos.com 14, 20, 41; Thyssen-Bornemisza Museum: 24; Topfoto: 23; Torsten Schleese: 21; Wolfgang Sauber: 37.

Brown Bear Books has made every attempt to contact the copyright holder.
If you have any information please contact licensing@brownbearbooks.co.uk

We believe the extracts included in this book to be material in the public domain.
Anyone having further information should contact licensing@brownbearbooks.co.uk

Printed in the United States of America

CONTENTS

INTRODUCTION

Primary sources are the best way to get close to people from the past. They include the things people wrote in diaries, letters, or books; the paintings, drawings, maps, or cartoons they created; and even the buildings they constructed, the clothes they wore, or the objects they owned. Such sources often reveal a lot about how people saw themselves and how they thought about their world.

This book collects a range of primary sources from a period of change known as the Reformation. The word describes a movement during the sixteenth and early seventeenth centuries when Europeans who had originally wanted to reform the Roman Catholic Church instead created a new branch of Christianity. There had been critics of the Catholic Church before the sixteenth century. In 1517, however, a protest by the German monk Martin Luther against church corruption led to the first form of Protestantism.

Lutheranism, as the new faith was called, spread quickly. Many of Europe's rulers adopted it as a way to challenge the authority of the pope in Rome. As Protestantism developed, the Catholic Church launched the Counter-Reformation. Parts of Europe were devastated by war as supporters of the two faiths fought for supremacy before the Peace of Westphalia in 1648 finally brought religious peace, allowing the faiths to coexist.

HOW TO USE THIS BOOK

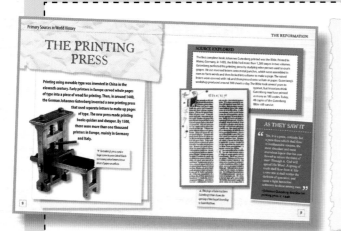

Each spread contains at least one primary source. Look out for "Source Explored" boxes that explain images from the Reformation and who made them and why. There are also "As They Saw It" boxes that contain quotes from people of the period.

Some boxes contain more detailed information about a particular aspect of a subject. The subjects are arranged in roughly chronological order. They focus on key events or people. There is a full timeline of the period at the back of the book.

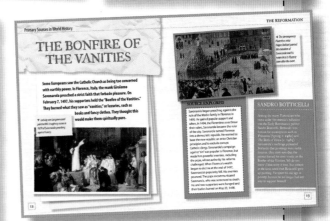

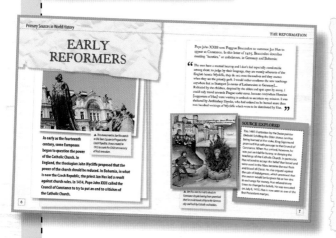

Some spreads feature a longer extract from a contemporary eyewitness. Look for the colored introduction that explains who the writer is and the origin of his or her account. These accounts are often accompanied by a related visual primary source.

EARLY REFORMERS

▲ *This monument to Jan Hus stands in Old Town Square in Prague in the Czech Republic. It was created in 1915 to mark the 500th anniversary of Hus's execution.*

As early as the fourteenth century, some Europeans began to question the power of the Catholic Church. In England, the theologian John Wycliffe proposed that the power of the church should be reduced. In Bohemia, in what is now the Czech Republic, the priest Jan Hus led a revolt against church rules. In 1414, John XXIII called the Council of Constance to try to put an end to criticism of the Catholic Church.

John XXIII sent Poggius Bracciolini to summon Jan Hus to appear at Constance. In this letter of 1415, Bracciolini describes meeting "heretics," or unbelievers, in Germany and Bohemia:

" The men have a martial bearing and I don't feel especially comfortable among them; to judge by their language, they are mostly adherents of the English heretic Wycliffe, they do not cross themselves and they mutter when they see the priestly garb. I would rather condemn the new teachings anywhere but in Stuttgart [a center of Lutheranism in Germany]. ... Ridiculed by the children, despised by the elders and spat upon by many, I could only travel towards Prague under cover, because everywhere Hussites [supporters of Hus] were waiting in ambush to ascertain my mission. I was sheltered by Archbishop Sbynko, who had ordered to be burned more than two hundred writings of Wycliffe which were to be distributed by Hus. "

▲ Jan Hus was burned to death in Constance despite having been promised that he could travel safely to the German city and back by Catholic authorities.

SOURCE EXPLORED

This 1485 illustration by the Swiss painter Diebold Schilling the Elder shows Jan Hus being burned at the stake. King Sigismund promised Hus safe passage to the Council of Constance. When Hus arrived, however, he was put on trial for heresy, or denying the teachings of the Catholic Church. In particular, Hus refused to accept the belief that bread and wine used in the Mass became the real flesh and blood of Christ. He also argued against the sale of indulgences, which promised that the owner would be forgiven his or her sins in exchange for money. Hus refused many times to change his beliefs. He was executed on July 6, 1415. Hus is now seen as one of the first Protestant martyrs.

THE PRINTING PRESS

Printing using movable type was invented in China in the eleventh century. Early printers in Europe carved whole pages of type into a piece of wood for printing. Then, in around 1440, the German Johannes Gutenberg invented a new printing press that used separate letters to make up pages of type. The new press made printing books quicker and cheaper. By 1500, there were more than one thousand printers throughout Europe.

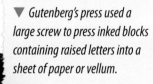

▼ *Gutenberg's press used a large screw to press inked blocks containing raised letters into a sheet of paper or vellum.*

...Gutenberg printed was the Bible. Printed in ...had more than 1,200 pages in two volumes. ...ess by studying wine presses used to crush ...metal punches, which were assembled in ...into a frame to make a page. The raised ...n pressed onto vellum or paper. Gutenberg's ...s a day. The Bible took several years to typeset, but historians think Gutenberg may have printed as many as 185 copies. Today, 48 copies of the Gutenberg Bible still survive.

▲ This page of Latin text from Gutenberg's Bible shows the opening of the Gospel According to Saint Matthew.

AS THEY SAW IT

" Yes, it is a press, certainly, but a press from which shall flow in inexhaustible streams, the most abundant and most marvelous liquor that has ever flowed to relieve the thirst of men! Through it, God will spread His Word. A spring of truth shall flow from it: like a new star it shall scatter the darkness of ignorance, and cause a light heretofore unknown to shine among men. "

—Johannes Gutenberg describes his printing press, circa 1440.

THE SPANISH INQUISITION

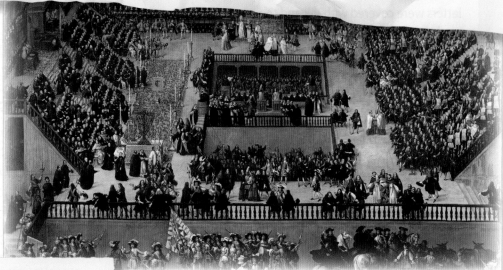

▲ *This 1683 painting by Francisco Rizi shows an auto-da-fé, or "act of faith," in Madrid. Those found guilty of heresy performed a public act of penance before being executed.*

In 1478, the Catholic rulers of Spain, Ferdinand II of Aragon and Isabella I of Castile, established the Inquisition. This was a body set up to fight heresy. It tried anyone who did not accept the teachings of the Catholic Church, such as Protestants, Muslims, or Jews. In 1492, all Jews who refused to become Christians were expelled from Spain. The Inquisition was known for its brutality. Under the monk Tomás de Torquemada, the grand inquisitor from 1483 to 1498, 2,000 people were burned at the stake for religious and other offenses.

◄ This nineteenth-century painting by Francisco Goya shows four convicted heretics (in dunce's hats) performing an auto-da-fé inside a church.

SOURCE EXPLORED

Under the Inquisition, anyone who was not a loyal Catholic could be taken in front of a religious court. The victims included heretics who rejected Catholic teaching and Jews. Later, they also included Protestants. The inquisitors who investigated their beliefs sometimes used torture in order to make them confess their guilt. Even children and old people could be tortured. If they were found guilty, the accused were forced to make a public act of penance called an auto-da-fé, or "act of faith." They might have to promise to give up their own beliefs and live as a Catholic. Those who refused to give up their beliefs were often publicly executed, usually by burning.

AS THEY SAW IT

" A prisoner in the Inquisition is never allowed to see the face of his accuser, or of the witnesses against him, but every method is taken by threats and tortures, to oblige him to accuse himself, and by that means corroborate their evidence. "

—In his *Book of Martyrs* (1563), the English Protestant John Foxe describes the operation of the Inquisition in Spain.

THE BONFIRE OF THE VANITIES

Some Europeans saw the Catholic Church as being too concerned with earthly power. In Florence, Italy, the monk Girolamo Savonarola preached a strict faith that forbade pleasure. On February 7, 1497, his supporters held the "Bonfire of the Vanities." They burned what they saw as "vanities," or luxuries, such as books and fancy clothes. They thought this would make them spiritually pure.

▼ Ludwig von Langenmantel painted this imaginary scene in 1879 of Savonarola preaching against luxury.

◀ *The contemporary Florentine artist Filippo Dolciati painted the execution of Savonarola and his supporters in Florence soon after the event.*

SOURCE EXPLORED

Savonarola began preaching against the rule of the Medici family in Florence in 1490. He gained popular support and when, in 1494, the Florentines overthrew their rulers, Savonarola became the ruler of the city. Savonarola turned Florence into a democratic republic. He wanted to base the new republic on strict Christian principles and to exclude corrupt Catholic clergy. Savonarola's campaign against "sin" was popular in Florence, but made him powerful enemies, including the pope, whose authority his reforms challenged. When Florence's wealth began to decline at the end of 1497, Savonarola's popularity fell. His enemies pounced. The pope excommunicated Savonarola, who was sentenced to death. He and two supporters were hanged and their bodies burned on May 23, 1498.

SANDRO BOTTICELLI

Among the many Florentines who came under Savonarola's influence was the Early Renaissance painter Sandro Botticelli. Botticelli was famous for masterpieces such as *Primavera* (Spring; ca. 1482) and *The Birth of Venus* (ca. 1485). Savonarola's teachings persuaded Botticelli that paintings were sinful luxuries. One story says that the painter burned his own works on the Bonfire of the Vanities. We do not know if that story is true, but writers at the time noted that Boticcelli gave up painting. He spent his old age in poverty, because he no longer had any way to support himself.

THE CHALLENGE OF SCIENCE

The Catholic Church taught that Earth was the center of the universe and that the Sun moved around it. That theory had been suggested in the second century BCE by the Greek astronomer Ptolemy. In the sixteenth century, astronomers began to challenge this theory. In 1543 the Polish astronomer Nicolaus Copernicus published his theory that the Earth revolved around the Sun.

▼ *These pages from Copernicus's book* De Revolutionibus *include a diagram that shows how the planets—including the Earth—orbit the Sun.*

Copernicus identified that the Earth orbited the Sun as early as 1510, but he did not publish his findings until 1543 because he knew the Catholic Church would not accept them. To try to avoid controversy, he dedicated *De Revolutionibus*, to Pope Paul III. Copernicus explained why he finally printed his revolutionary theories:

> **"** I can well believe that, when what I have written becomes known, there will be an uproar ... The fear of the ridicule which must needs be called forth by the novelty and apparent absurdity of my system had determined me to abstain from publishing my work. The insistence of my friends, however ... overcame my disinclination ... [They] insisted that I should print this book, which has been in preparation, not nine only, but thirty-six years ... After long study I came to these conclusions: that the sun is a fixed star, surrounded by planets which revolve round it and of which it is the center and the light. **"**

SOURCE EXPLORED

These notes were written by the Italian scientist Galileo Galilei in 1610 to record his discovery of the four moons of Jupiter, which he made using a telescope.

The telescope had been invented in 1608 in the Netherlands. When Galileo heard about it, he built his own, improved telescope to allow him to observe the night sky. His discovery of moons orbiting Jupiter went against church teaching, in which all objects in the heavens were said to orbit the Earth. Galileo also studied the motion of the planets. He agreed with Copernicus that the Earth orbited the Sun. The Inquisition put him on trial for heresy. He was forced to deny his theories and was sentenced to house arrest. He remained a prisoner until his death in 1642.

▲ Galileo's discovery of the moons of Jupiter showed for the first time that space contained objects invisible to the naked eye.

THE INDULGENCE CRISIS

The Catholic Church taught that people who committed certain types of sin went to Purgatory after death, where their souls were purified before they entered Heaven. In the Middle Ages, the church began selling "indulgences." These promised an end of temporal punishment for forgiven sins. Some people were against indulgences, saying they allowed the rich to buy forgiveness for their sins. By the 1500s, however, the church was also selling indulgences as a way to raise money.

◄ The main purpose of the sale of indulgences under Pope Leo X was to raise money for rebuilding St. Peter's Church in the Vatican. Leo X became known for his extravagant spending on artists and architects.

SOURCE EXPLORED

In this nineteenth-century painting by Johann Daniel Wagner, the German friar named Johann Tetzel sells indulgences in a town in Germany in the early 1500s. In 1513, Giovanni de' Medici became Pope Leo X. He was famous for his extravagant lifestyle. He wanted to make St. Peter's Basilica in the Vatican the most magnificent church in the world. He decided to fund the project by selling indulgences and asked Tetzel to sell more indulgences in Germany. Tetzel's drive to raise money angered many people. One of them was the monk Martin Luther, who strongly protested against Tetzel's actions.

AS THEY SAW IT

66 Tetzel gained by his preaching in Germany an immense sum of money which he sent to Rome... It is incredible what this ignorant and impudent monk used to say... He declared that as soon as the coin clinked in the chest, the soul for whom the money was paid would go straight to heaven ... He was conducted into the church, a red cross was erected in the center of the church and the pope's banner displayed... 99

—Priest Frederick Mecum reports on Johann Tetzel preaching in 1512.

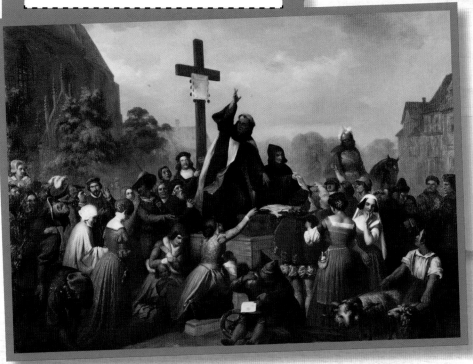

◀ Daniel Wagner's painting shows Tetzel preaching next to the red cross that he always erected as he traveled around Germany.

MARTIN LUTHER AND THE 95 THESES

Martin Luther was born in Germany in 1483. His father wanted him to train as a lawyer, but Luther soon gave up the law. In 1505 he entered a monastery and became a monk. On a visit to Rome in 1510, he was shocked by the corruption he saw in the Catholic Church. In 1513 he began to object to Johann Tetzel's sale of indulgences in Germany. In 1517 Luther began a protest against such practices. His protest would lead to the creation of a new branch of Christianity: Protestantism.

▶ *This portrait of Martin Luther is one of a number painted by the German artist Lucas Cranach, Luther's close supporter.*

◀ *This print from 1874 celebrates the lives of Protestant heroes of the Reformation. In the center, Martin Luther burns the document excommunicating him from the Catholic Church.*

SOURCE EXPLORED

On October 31, 1517, Martin Luther nailed a document known as the "95 Theses" to the door of the Castle Church in Wittenberg, Germany. At the time, this was a recognized way to start a debate. Luther also sent a copy of the document to the local archbishop. It was a list in Latin of 95 objections against the Catholic Church, most of which were concerned with the selling of indulgences and the pope's abuse of his power. Luther argued that it was better to sell St. Peter's than to ask the poor to buy indulgences to pay for its expansion. In early 1518, Luther's supporters translated the theses into German. Thanks to new printing technology, his ideas soon spread across Europe. Luther became the leader of a movement to change the Catholic Church.

AS THEY SAW IT

" I only intended submitting [the theses] to a few learned men for examination, and if they disapproved of them, to suppress them—or make them known through their publications, in the event of their meeting with your approval. But now they are being spread abroad and translated everywhere ... I regret having given birth to them—not that I am unwilling to proclaim the truth manfully ... but because this way of instructing the people is of little avail. "

—Martin Luther writes to the German diplomat Christoph von Scheurl on March 5, 1518.

LUTHER'S TEACHINGS

▲ This engraving shows Luther burning a bull, or papal letter, threatening to excommunicate him from the Catholic Church on December 10, 1520.

Luther only intended to begin a debate rather than start a new church. However, in January 1521 he was excommunicated, meaning he could not receive the sacraments. Luther was protected by a local ruler in Wartburg Castle, Germany. There he developed his ideas about faith. He said people were justified, or found salvation, by faith alone. They would not find it through buying indulgences or doing good works. Luther also thought people should be able to read the word of God themselves in the Bible rather than being told by priests what it meant.

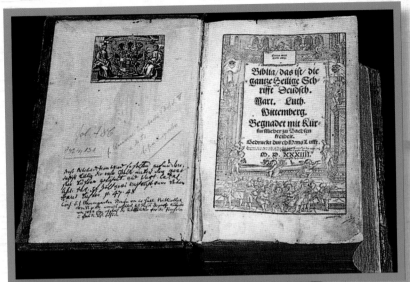

◀ Luther's Bible was published in 1534, but he had translated the New Testament into German over a decade earlier.

SOURCE EXPLORED

One of the most important reforms Luther called for was for the Bible to be accessible to ordinary people. That meant it needed to be in local languages, rather than Latin or Greek. While in Wartburg Castle in 1521, he spent nine months translating the New Testament from Hebrew and Greek into German. Luther's complete Bible was printed in 1534. Large numbers soon appeared, thanks to the many printing presses in Germany. The Bible was welcomed across Germany. Not only could many Germans now read it for themselves for the first time. It also had political appeal. Germany was then a series of states that belonged to the Holy Roman Empire. Some German princes saw Luther's teachings as a means to break away from the control of the empire, which was loyal to the Catholic Church.

AS THEY SAW IT

" The deplorable conditions which I recently encountered ... constrained me to prepare this brief and simple catechism [teaching manual] ... What wretchedness I beheld! The common people, especially those who live in the country, have no knowledge whatever of Christian teaching ... How will you bishops answer for it before Christ that you have so shamefully neglected the people and paid no attention at all to the duties of your office? "

—Luther explains why he wrote the *Small Catechism* (1529), his first textbook for children.

REFORMATION IN SWITZERLAND

From Germany, Luther's idea that people could find salvation through faith alone spread to neighboring Switzerland. In Zürich, the preacher Huldrych Zwingli supported the new teachings. The split between Zwingli's followers and Swiss Catholics led to the Wars of Kappel in 1529 and again in 1531. The Catholic states were victorious, so Protestantism remained limited to about a third of Swiss cantons.

▼ *Zwingli was an important reformer in the city of Zürich, where the city adopted his teachings about faith.*

SOURCE EXPLORED

The Swiss artist Hans Asper painted this portrait of Huldrych Zwingli in 1549, eighteen years after Zwingli's death. Like Luther, Zwingli opposed the sale of indulgences, but he also introduced his own reforms. In 1522, he allowed his parishioners to eat meat during Lent, when it was forbidden by the Catholic Church. Zwingli also argued that priests should not remain unmarried, and himself married in 1524. He questioned the importance of Mass and called for statues to be removed from churches. Although Zwingli was condemned as a heretic, the city council of Zürich adopted his beliefs as its official faith in 1523. Zwingli died in 1531 fighting against the Catholic cantons in the Second War of Kappel.

HVLDRYCHVS ZVINGLIVS,
DVM PATRIÆ QVÆRO PER DOGMATA SANCTA SALVTEM,
INGRATO PATRIÆ CÆSVS AB ENSE CADO,

OBIIT AÑO DÑI, M.D.XXXI, OCDOB,
ÆTATIS SVÆ, XLVIII,   H

▲ *Zwingli believed people should read the Bible to learn God's teachings for themselves, rather than rely on Catholic priests to explain the Bible to them.*

MEETING LUTHER

Zwingli and Martin Luther had one serious difference of belief. Zwingli believed that the bread and wine used during Mass were simply symbols of Christ's body and blood. Luther believed that they actually became the real body and blood of Christ. In October 1529 the two men met at the German town of Marburg to discuss their differences with other leading reformers. The Colloquy (debate) of Marburg lasted four days. The two men could not reach agreement, however. They never met again.

REFORMATION IN ENGLAND

▲ Henry VIII forced the Archbishop of Canterbury, Thomas Cranmer, to allow him to divorce Catherine of Aragon despite the objections of the Pope in Rome.

In England, King Henry VIII had personal reasons to break away from the Catholic Church. He had married Catherine of Aragon in 1509, but they had not had a male heir. Meanwhile, Henry had decided to marry Anne Boleyn. When the pope refused to allow Henry to divorce Catherine, the king ignored him. He married Anne Boleyn in January 1533. The Act of Supremacy of 1534 made Henry head of a new church, the Church of England. In 1538 the Pope excommunicated Henry. When Henry's daughter, Mary, became queen in 1553, she reintroduced Catholicism. When Mary's half-sister, Elizabeth I, took the throne in 1558, she reintroduced the Church of England.

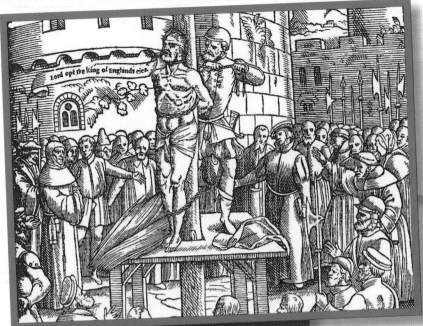

◀ *This illustration shows William Tyndale just before his death in 1536. The speech bubble contains his last words, "Lord, open the King of England's eyes."*

SOURCE EXPLORED

This woodcut from 1563 shows the English religious reformer William Tyndale being executed for heresy in 1536. Born in the late 1480s or early 1490s, Tyndale learned many languages. He became a priest and began to argue that an English translation of the Bible was needed. In 1523, he began to translate the New Testament into English, although this was illegal in the Catholic country. Tyndale believed that the Bible should be the basis of a person's faith and that it must be in English so that Englishmen could read it rather than rely on priests to translate the Latin versions. He fled to Germany. Copies of his English Bible were smuggled into England in 1526. He was later arrested in the Catholic Low Countries, tried for heresy, and executed.

THOMAS MORE

The humanist scholar Thomas More was one of Henry's close advisors. In 1529 he became Lord High Chancellor of England, one of the most important royal officials. More rejected the teachings of Martin Luther and William Tyndale. He opposed Henry's decision to leave the Catholic Church and did not accept that he could divorce Catherine of Aragon. He believed the king had to obey the spiritual authority of the pope. After the Act of Supremacy in 1534, More refused to acknowledge Henry as the head of the new Church of England. More was tried and found guilty of treason. He was beheaded on July 6, 1535. The Catholic Church made him a saint in 1935.

DISSOLUTION OF THE MONASTERIES

Under the Catholic Church, England's monasteries and convents had grown wealthy. Some people criticized the desire of the monks and nuns to make money. After he became head of the Church of England, Henry VIII closed the Catholic monasteries. This was a signal that Catholicism was no longer welcome in England. It also gained land and money for the crown.

▼ The cloister at Lacock Abbey in southern Britain was used by monks as a quiet place where they could walk quietly and think about questions of faith.

▲ *The Cistercian abbey at Tintern was founded in 1131.*

SOURCE EXPLORED

Tintern Abbey stands in ruins on the border between England and Wales. The abbey was home to Cistercian monks for about four hundred years until its abbot surrendered to soldiers sent by Henry VIII on September 3, 1536. Between 1536 and 1541, Henry VIII closed down all nine hundred or so monasteries and convents in England, Wales, and Ireland. Henry's supporters said that these religious houses, as they were known, were symbols of the unacceptable wealth, privilege, and greed of the Roman Catholic Church. Henry sold the vast land holdings, artworks, and gold and silver he gained from the dissolution of the monasteries. He used his new wealth to finance his military campaigns.

THE MONASTERIES

Monasteries were an important part of the economy. They received donations from local patrons and owned large areas of land that was rented to farmers to raise money for the monks. Many monasteries became centers for local industries such as brewing. They were also centers of literacy where monks and lay people learned to read. Monks spent much of their time reading or making hand-written copies of the Bible and other religious texts. These copies were kept in monastery libraries for other monks to study.

BLOODY MARY

King Henry VIII died in 1547. He was succeeded on the throne by his son, Edward VI. When Edward died in 1553, aged just fifteen, the crown passed to his step-sister, Mary Tudor. Mary was Henry's daughter by his first wife, Catherine of Aragon.

Like her mother, Mary was a devout Catholic. She returned England to the Catholic Church and put leading Protestant churchmen on trial for heresy. More than 280 Protestants were executed during Mary's five-year reign, earning her the nickname of "Bloody Mary."

◀ The Netherlandish artist Antonis Mor painted this portrait of Queen Mary I in 1554. Mor worked widely for the Hapsburg family, including Mary's husband, the Spanish king Philip II.

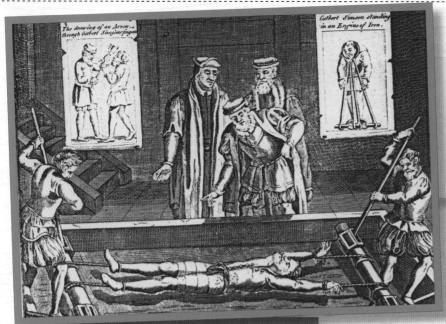

◀ In the background of this woodcut showing the torture of Cuthbert Simpson on the rack are scenes of other tortures that were also inflicted on him by Mary's officials.

SOURCE EXPLORED

This woodcut from 1563 shows an English Protestant named Cuthbert Simpson being tortured for attending an illegal church during the reign of Queen Mary. Despite being stretched on the rack, he would not reveal the names of his fellow worshipers. When he refused to recant, or give up, his faith, Simpson was sentenced to death for heresy. On March 28, 1558, he was burned at the stake. Many people had welcomed Mary's restoration of Catholicism, because they found Henry VIII's religious reforms too extreme. But such treatment of Protestants made Mary deeply unpopular, as did her marriage to the Catholic King Philip II of Spain. News of her death in 1558 was greeted with cheers in the streets of London.

AS THEY SAW IT

66 She is so confirmed in the Catholic religion that although the King her brother and his Council prohibited her from having Mass celebrated according to the Roman Catholic ritual, she nevertheless had it performed in secret, nor did she ever choose by any act to assent to any other form of religion... 99

—The Venetian ambassador in London reports on Queen Mary's devotion to her Catholic faith, August 18, 1554.

THE SOLDIERS OF CHRIST

The Spanish soldier Ignatius Loyola was wounded during a battle against the French in 1521. During his recovery, he decided to devote his life to Christ. In 1534 he and six companions

took vows of poverty and obedience to the pope. In 1540, Loyola founded the Society of Jesus to help resist the spread of the Protestant Reformation. He organized his followers, called Jesuits, with the same kind of discipline as soldiers. They became missionaries who preached Catholicism around the world.

◀ *This statue of Ignatius of Loyola stands in a church in San José de Chiquitos in Bolivia. Ignatius was made a saint in 1622.*

SOURCE EXPLORED

This illustration of Jesuit missionaries in China comes from a Jesuit history published in 1735. It includes Matteo Ricci (top left), who became a close advisor to the Chinese emperor. Like other Jesuit missionaries, Ricci learned to speak the local language and adopted local customs. Loyola taught that the best way to spread Catholicism was through education, so Jesuit missionaries set up schools, universities, and colleges overseas. They were particularly active in the Americas and East Asia. When Loyola died in 1556, there were more than 1,000 Jesuits. By 1626, there were 15,000 Jesuits and 440 colleges throughout the world.

AS THEY SAW IT

"With him there was no such thing as feeling his pulse, no taking a reckoning by the North Star, no steering by a sea chart, as is the usual way of dealing with men in authority, for he was always in a state of calm self-mastery."

—Pedro de Ribadeneira, who became a Jesuit in 1540, describes the personality of Ignatius Loyola.

◀ This illustration shows three Jesuit missionaries in China (top), including Matteo Ricci, holding instruments associated with Western astronomy. The lower half of the image shows a cross together with two Chinese converts to Catholicism.

JOHN CALVIN

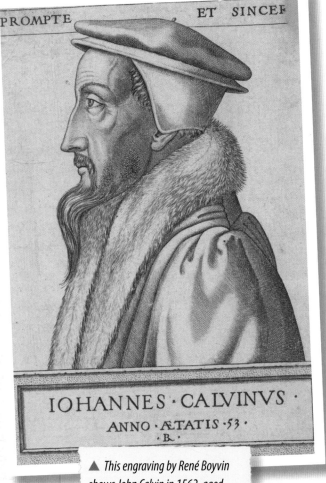

PROMPTE   ET SINCER

IOHANNES · CALVINVS ·
ANNO · ÆTATIS ·53·
·B·

▲ This engraving by René Boyvin shows John Calvin in 1562, aged fifty-three. Calvin spent his later years setting up a college in Geneva and teaching his beliefs.

John Calvin was born in 1509 in Picardy, France. He studied law in Paris until a religious conversion in 1533 convinced him to dedicate his life to Protestantism. Forced to flee France for his views, he was based in Geneva, Switzerland, from 1536. There, Calvin tried to create a society based on "godly behavior." He preached that individuals must read the Bible for themselves in order to understand God's word. Geneva became the center of his strict form of Protestantism, which is known as Calvinism.

SOURCE EXPLORED

This is a facsimile of a letter by Calvin dated July 4, 1552. It is one of a number of letters Calvin wrote to Edward VI, the young King of England who ruled for six years after the death of Henry VIII in 1547. Calvin tried to convince Edward to do what he could to help Protestantism flourish. Calvin also wrote to many of Europe's other rulers to encourage them to adopt Protestantism and he dedicated his book, *Institutes of the Christian Religion*, to Francis I, the King of France. Like Luther, Calvin stressed that people should have a direct relationship with God, without interference from priests. For this reason, he said people should study the Bible themselves. This was now easier because the Bible had been translated into many European languages.

Fac Simile

CALVIN TO EDWARD VI, KING OF ENGLAND.

July 4 1552 — British Museum.

▲ Calvin wrote to many of Europe's rulers in order to spread Protestantism. His strict views inspired later Protestant groups in countries such as Scotland.

AS THEY SAW IT

❝ Geneva, where I neither fear man nor am ashamed to say that this is the most perfect school of Christ that ever was in the earth since the days of the apostles. In other places, I confess Christ to be truly preached; but manners and religion to be so sincerely reformed, I have not yet seen in any other place. ❞

—Scottish Protestant John Knox describes a visit he made to Geneva in December 1556.

THE FRENCH WARS OF RELIGION

▲ Armed members of the French Holy League parade through Paris in 1590. The League was formed to defend France from Protestantism.

Between 1562 and 1598, France was torn apart by a series of wars between Protestants, or Huguenots, and Catholics, who made up most of the population. The clash was influenced by politics. Protestant nobles wanted to challenge the power of the French crown, which supported the Catholic Church. In the Edict of Nantes in 1598, King Henry IV of France granted freedom of worship to the Huguenots, who followed the teachings of John Calvin. Henry's grandson, Louis XIV, overturned the edict in 1685, causing many Huguenots to leave France.

◀ In the background of his painting Dubois shows Catherine de Médici leaving the Louvre Palace in order to inspect the bodies of the murdered Huguenots.

SOURCE EXPLORED

This painting by Francois Dubois shows Huguenots being massacred by Catholics in Paris on St. Bartholomew's Day, August 24, 1572. The massacre was one of the worst incidents of the French Wars of Religion. The French Queen Mother, Catherine de Médici, is said to have encouraged the killing of prominent Huguenots after a plot to kill the Protestant leader Admiral de Coligny failed. King Charles IX ordered the deaths of about two hundred Huguenots who had gathered in Paris for the wedding of his sister, Margaret. Catholic mobs attacked Huguenots throughout Paris and across France. Up to five thousand victims died. Many Huguenots fled France, with many settling in London, England, and in Belgium. They founded important weaving industries in both countries.

AS THEY SAW IT

" There were madmen running to and fro, smashing down doors and shouting, 'Kill, kill, massacre the Huguenots.' Blood spattered before my eyes and doubled my fear. I ran into a clump of soldiers, who stopped me. They plied me with questions and began to jostle me about when luckily they saw my breviary [Catholic prayer book]. "

—The thirteen-year-old Duke of Sully, who later bcame an advisor to King Henry IV, describes how he escaped the massacre.

35

THE COUNCIL OF TRENT

▲ One target of the Council of Trent was the spread of fraudulent relics. This silver urn in a church in Rome is claimed to contain wood from Jesus's crib from Bethlehem.

In the face of the Protestant Reformation, the Catholic Church summoned its senior churchmen to a meeting in the town of Trent, in the Italian Alps. The Council of Trent lasted on and off from 1545 to 1563 as the Catholics planned a response to the new religion. The council clarified points of Catholic doctrine and imposed new rules on parts of worship, such as church music. The result was a Catholic Church that was more energized for the Counter-Reformation, its ongoing fight against the spread of Protestantism.

The Council of Trent published "A decree on the Invocation, Veneration, and Relics, of Saints, and on Sacred Images" on December 3, 1563. The decree tried to prevent the veneration of relics—the superstitious worship of the remains or possessions of holy people of the past:

> **"** And if any abuses have crept in amongst these holy observances, the holy Synod ardently desires that they be utterly abolished; in such wise that no images, [suggestive] of false doctrine, and furnishing occasion of dangerous error to the uneducated, be set up. And if at times, when expedient for the unlettered people; it happen that the facts and narratives of sacred Scripture are portrayed and represented; the people shall be taught, that not thereby is the Divinity represented, as though it could be seen by the eyes of the body, or be portrayed by colors or figures. **"**

SOURCE EXPLORED

This painting shows the Council of Trent in session. In the center is Pope Paul III, who called the council's first session. Along with the pope, the attendees included cardinals, bishops, and leading Catholic theologians. No Protestants attended. In 1545, when the Council began, the Christian church was still theoretically united. By the time it ended in 1563, it had split into two branches. The Catholic Church made it clear that it would not adopt any of the beliefs of Protestantism.

▲ *The Council of Trent was the Catholic Church's formal response to the Reformation. It confirmed the basics of Catholic belief, rejecting the arguments of Protestants.*

THE COUNTER-REFORMATION

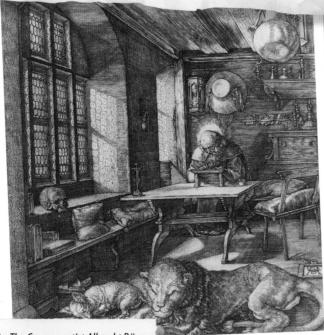

▲ The German artist Albrecht Dürer made this engraving of Saint Jerome in 1514. The Catholic Church saw the arts as an important way to communicate and spread the faith.

The Counter-Reformation that followed the Council of Trent reformed the Catholic Church to better challenge the growing power of Protestant churches. The Catholic Church was still popular in many parts of Europe. The Counter-Reformation removed abuses such as the mass sale of indulgences. It gave the pope more spiritual authority, reformed old religious orders, and created new ones, such as the Jesuits. The church hired many artists and architects to join a program of building and decorating churches.

SOURCE EXPLORED

The Italian artist Paulo Veronese painted *The Battle of Lepanto* in around 1572. The previous year, an alliance of Catholic powers had defeated the Muslim Ottoman Turks in a sea battle near Cyprus. The Holy League included Spain, the Papacy, Venice, and Genoa. Its ships won a decisive victory over the Turks on October 7, 1571, stopping Ottoman influence spreading in the Mediterranean Sea. Veronese's painting was created to hang in the Doge's Palace in Venice. It reflects the new confidence of the Catholic Church. It attributes the victory of the Holy League ships, at the bottom of the painting, to the divine intervention of the Virgin Mary and saints, at the top.

▲ *The top half of Veronese's painting shows a female figure representing Venice being presented to the Virgin Mary, surrounded by saints and angels.*

AS THEY SAW IT

" Hurtling towards each other, the two fleets were a quite terrifying sight: our men in shining helmets and breastplates, metal shields like mirrors and their other weapons glittering in the rays of the sun, the polished blades of the drawn swords dazzling men full in the face even from a distance ... and the enemy were no less threatening, they struck just as much fear in the hearts of our side, as well as amazement and wonder at the golden lanterns and shimmering banners... "

—The Venetian Girolamo Diedo describes the Battle of Lepanto.

THE SPANISH ARMADA

In 1558 Elizabeth I took the English throne after the death of her half-sister, Mary Tudor, and restored the Protestant faith. Mary's husband, King Philip II of Spain, was a devout Catholic who wanted England to remain a Catholic country. In 1588, he sent a powerful Armada, or fleet, to invade England. He wanted to prevent English sea captains such as Francis Drake from raiding Spanish colonies in the Caribbean Sea. The invasion failed after the English fleet defeated the Spaniards in the English Channel.

ELIZABETHA ANGLIÆ ET HIBERNIÆ REGINÆ. &c.

◀ Queen Elizabeth I encouraged her sailors in a famous speech in which she said, "I know I have the body but of a weak and feeble woman, but I have the heart and stomach of a king—and of a king of England, too."

▲ *This painting shows the confused fighting between Spanish and English ships.*

An unknown artist painted the English and Spanish fleets clashing near Calais, France. The Armada usually fought in a long, crescent-shaped line, but the English used their more powerful cannon to disrupt the Spanish ships. They also set old ships on fire and sailed them toward the Spaniards, who had to flee. The winds turned against the Spanish ships, which were unable to get back into position. With many vessels destroyed, the surviving Spanish ships fled. Some headed north through the North Sea to sail around the top of Scotland. Many were destroyed by storms on the way back to Spain.

Sir John Hawkins was an English naval commander in the battle against the 130-vessel Spanish fleet. In a letter dated July 31, 1588, he describes what happened:

" We followed the Spaniards, and all that day had with them a long and great fight, wherein there was great valor showed generally of our company. In this battle, there was spent very much of our powder and shot; and so the wind began to blow westerly, a fresh gale, and the Spaniards put themselves somewhat to the northward, where we follow and keep company with them. In this fight there were some hurt done among the Spaniards. A great ship of the galleons of Portugal, her rudder spoiled, and so the fleet left her in the sea.... Our ships, God be thanked, have received little hurt... "

THE THIRTY YEARS' WAR

▲ *Protestant nobles in Bohemia throw Catholic ambassadors out of a palace window. The incident sparked the Thirty Years' War.*

In 1617, Ferdinand of Styria was elected by the Diet, or parliament, of Bohemia as king. Most Bohemians were Protestant, however, while Ferdinand was a devout Catholic. In 1618 fighting began between followers of the two faiths. A system of alliances led to a war that grew to include most of Europe. The conflict ended in 1648, with the signing of the Peace of Westphalia. The treaty allowed Europe's princes to decide the religion of their own territories: Catholicism, Lutheranism, or Calvinism. Members of minority religions would be allowed to worship in private without persecution.

The Thirty Years' War brought devastation to much of central Europe. Here Gallus Zembroth, mayor of Allensbach in Switzerland, describes what happened when Spanish troops (who were on his side) occupied the town in 1640:

" They stayed here eight long weeks and created havoc. They tore down some 20 houses and wine-press buildings, and smashed up many others so they were no longer habitable... They used all the hay, of which there was a good quantity, for fodder, and took what there was in the neighborhood away... More than 200 horses collapsed from hunger and died. Many tens of acres of vines, together with all the stakes and fences, were burned. Some of the cattle were taken away at the beginning by the soldiers and the rest were slaughtered. There was such devastation that it can scarcely be described, as apart from burning the village nothing else was spared us. **"**

▲ The Flemish painter Sebastian Vrancx was a specialist in war painting who often depicted the effects of conflict on ordinary Europeans.

SOURCE EXPLORED

This 1647 painting by Sebastian Vrancx shows soldiers robbing and killing travelers in a landscape devastated by war. The Thirty Years' War was catastrophic for many ordinary Europeans. As well as widespread fighting, soldiers also roamed central Europe in lawless gangs, stealing from local communities. Some seven million Europeans died during the war, not only from violence but also from starvation or disease. The vast majority of the casualties were civilians.

TIMELINE

1415	**July 6:** Jan Hus is executed in what is now the Czech Republic for challenging the beliefs of the Catholic Church.
ca. 1440	Johannes Gutenberg introduces the first European printing press with moveable, or reusable, type. His invention speeds up the production of books and the spread of new ideas in Europe.
1478	The Spanish rulers, Ferdinand and Isabella, introduce the Spanish Inquisition to oppose heresy in Spain; the Inquisition is later established in Spain's empire in America.
1492	Spain expels all Jews who refuse to convert to Christianity.
1497	**February 7:** In Florence, Italy, followers of the monk Girolamo Savonarola hold a "bonfire of the vanities," burning any possessions they associate with sin and indulgence.
1513	Giovanni de Lorenzo de' Medici becomes pope as Leo X. He plans to renovate St. Peter's Church in the Vatican using funds raised by selling indulgences.
1517	**October 31:** The German monk Martin Luther posts his 95 Theses on the door of a church in Wittenberg, listing his objections to the sale of indulgences and other corruption within the Catholic Church.
1521	Luther meets the Pope at the Diet of Worms, where he refuses to withdraw his objections. He is charged with heresy and excommunicated, but is protected by a local ruler who holds him in Wartburg Castle for his own safety.
1522	Luther translates the New Testament of the Bible into German.
1523	The city council of Zürich in Switzerland adopts the reformist beliefs of Huldrych Zwingli as the city's official faith.
1526	William Tyndale publishes the first English translation of the Bible.
1529	Martin Luther meets Huldrych Zwingli at Marburg, but they are unable to agree on the meaning of the celebration of Mass.
1530	The beliefs and practices of Lutheranism are outlined in the Augsburg Confession.
1531	**October 11:** Zwingli dies during the Second War of Kappel, which leaves Switzerland split between Protestant and Catholic cantons.
1534	**August 15:** The Spanish monk Ignatius of Loyola and his companions take vows of loyalty to the Catholic Church.

1534	**November:** The Act of Supremacy makes King Henry VIII head of the Church of England, which splits from the Roman Catholic Church.
1535	**July 6:** The English scholar and statesman Thomas More is executed for refusing to reject the Catholic Church.
1536	William Tyndale is executed for heresy. Henry VIII begins the dissolution of the monasteries. French reformer John Calvin publishes his theological beliefs.
1545	Senior figures of the Catholic Church meet at the Council of Trent to clarify Catholic beliefs.
1553	Mary Tudor comes to the English throne and restores Catholicism, persecuting and executing leading Protestants.
1555	**September 25:** The Peace of Augsburg promises tolerance to Protestants within the Holy Roman Empire.
1562	Violence breaks out between Catholics and Protestants in France, beginning a long series of religious wars.
1563	The Council of Trent ends with the publication of guidelines about the beliefs and practices of the Catholic Church.
1572	**August 24:** Hundreds of leading French Protestants are massacred by Catholics in Paris on St. Bartholomew's Day.
1588	**July 29:** An English fleet defeats the Spanish Armada, which King Philip II has sent to support an invasion of England in order to restore the Catholic faith there.
1598	**April 30:** King Henry IV of France promises tolerance to French Protestants in the Edict of Nantes.
1618	**May 23:** Ambassadors of the new Catholic king of Protestant Bohemia are thrown out of a window in the castle of Prague. This "defenestration" marks the start of a widespread European conflict, the Thirty Years' War.
1648	The Thirty Years' War ends in the Peace of Westphalia. The treaty gives Europe's rulers power to establish the religion of their own territory, but provides that religious minorities should be allowed to practice their faith in private.

GLOSSARY

auto-da-fé An act of penance before being burned as a heretic by the Spanish Inquisition.

canton A state of Switzerland.

cardinals The most senior churchmen of the Catholic Church, who are appointed by the pope.

clergy Everyone qualified to carry out services in the Christian church.

cloister A covered walkway in a religious building.

decree An official order that has the power of law.

devout Describes someone with a deep religious faith.

dissolution The formal ending of an official body.

doctrine The set beliefs of a Church.

excommunicated Forbidden from taking Mass in the Catholic Church, which is effectively a ban from the religion.

facsimile A precise copy of an original document.

heir Someone who inherits property or a title on the death of another person.

heresy Beliefs that do not agree with the official doctrine of a Church.

heretic Someone who does not accept the doctrine of a Church.

humanist Someone who follows the ideas of humanism, which emphasizes secular or earthly matters and says problems can be solved using reason instead of religion.

indulgence A remission of temporal punishment for forgiven sins under defined conditions.

inquisition A religious court set up to uncover and eliminate heresy.

martyr Someone who dies for their religious beliefs or another cause.

Mass A service in which Catholics hear readings from the Bible and celebrate the Eucharist, or communion.

penance Self punishment carried out to express sorrow for doing something wrong.

persecution The mistreatment of a group of people for their beliefs, ethnicity, or other reasons.

Purgatory A state of suffering by the souls of sinners after death as they wait to enter Heaven.

religious orders Societies of monks or nuns who live according to particular rules.

republic A state in which people vote for a government to represent them.

spiritual Relating to the human soul, beliefs, and spirit rather than to everyday concerns.

theologian Someone who studies religious beliefs and practices.

theses Statements or theories that are put forward to begin a debate.

worldliness An approach to life that places more emphasis on physical concerns than on spiritual concerns.

FURTHER INFORMATION

Books

Childress, Diana. *Johannes Gutenberg and the Printing Press*. Pivotal Moments in History. Minneapolis: Twenty-First Century Books, 2007.

Crompton, Samuel Willard. *Martin Luther*. Spiritual Leaders and Thinkers. Philadelphia: Chelsea House Publications, 2004.

Hollingsworth, Tamara. *The Reformation: A Religious Revolution*. Primary Source Readers: World History. Huntington Beach, CA: Teacher Created Materials, 2012.

Malam, John. *You Wouldn't Want to Sail in the Spanish Armada: An Invasion You'd Rather Not Launch*. New York: Franklin Watts, 2007.

Whitelaw, Nancy. *Catherine de' Medici and the Protestant Reformation*. Greensboro, NC: Morgan Reynolds Publishing, 2005.

Woog, Adam. *Life During the Spanish Inquisition*. Living History. San Diego, CA: Reference Point Press, 2014.

Websites

www.bbc.co.uk/history/british/tudors/english_reformation_01.shtml
A BBC site about the Tudors and the English Reformation.

www.encyclopedia.com/topic/Thirty_Years_War.aspx
An article about the history of the Thirty Year's War.

www.history.com/topics/reformation
An overview of the Reformation from History.com, with links and videos.

www.pbs.org/empires/medici/renaissance/counter.html
A page about the Catholic Counter-Reformation from a site supporting the PBS series on the Renaissance.

Publisher's note to educators and parents: Our editors have carefully reviewed these websites to ensure that they are suitable for students. Many websites change frequently, however, and we cannot guarantee that a site's future contents will continue to meet our high standards of quality and educational value. Be advised that students should be closely supervised whenever they access the Internet.

INDEX